Sex Coupons

For Her

From :

To Love,

GOOD FOR ONE

LET'S HAVE SEX IN FRONT OF MIRROR

GOOD FOR ONE

SENSUAL MASSAGE

AND THEN,.....

GOOD FOR ONE

YOUR BRA

BOTHER ME !

TAKE IT OF

ALL THE NIGHT

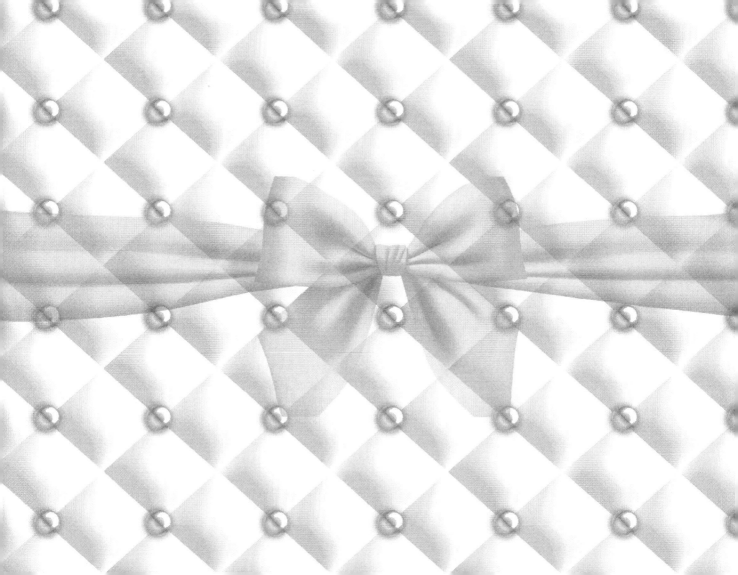

GOOD FOR ONE

SEX

IN

NEW PLACE

GOOD FOR ONE

LONG

FRENCH

KISS

GOOD FOR ONE

WHIP CREAM

OR

CHOCOLATE

SOME

ADVENTURE

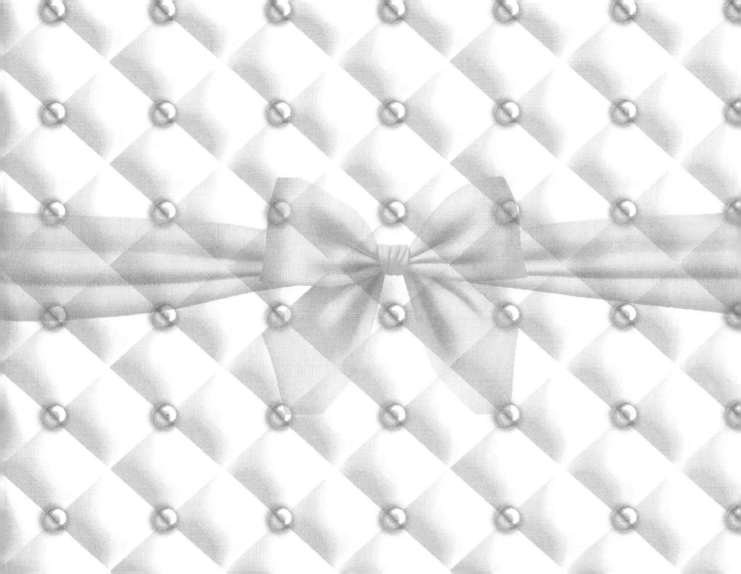

GOOD FOR ONE

STRIP POKER

GAME

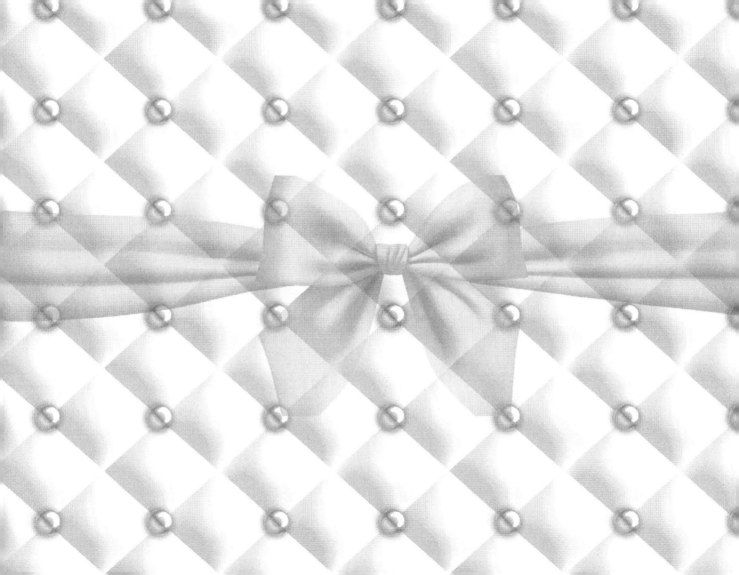

GOOD FOR ONE

SLEEP IN YOUR LAP

AND

YOUR NIPPLES

IN MY MOUTH

ALL THE NIGHT

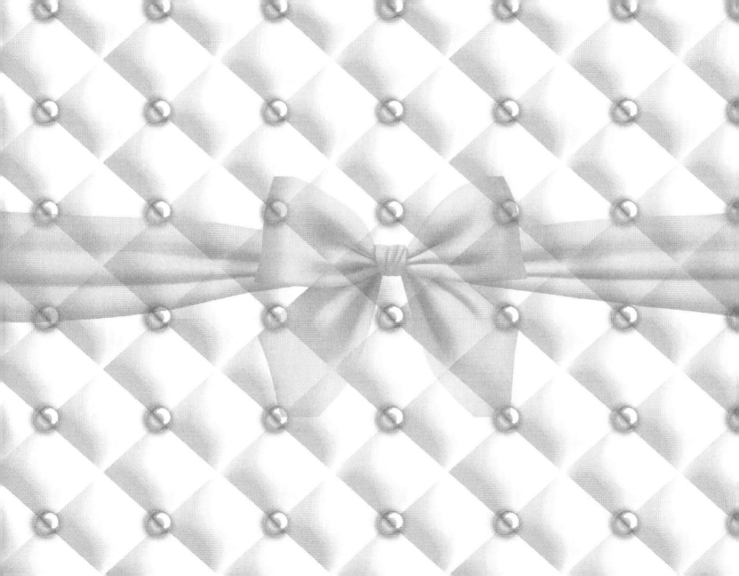

GOOD FOR ONE

A SKINNY DIPPING

ADVENTURE

GOOD FOR ONE

A STEAMY

MORNING BATH

FOR TWO

GOOD FOR ONE

LET'S DO IT

SLOWLY

GOOD FOR ONE

A DIRTY

DANCE

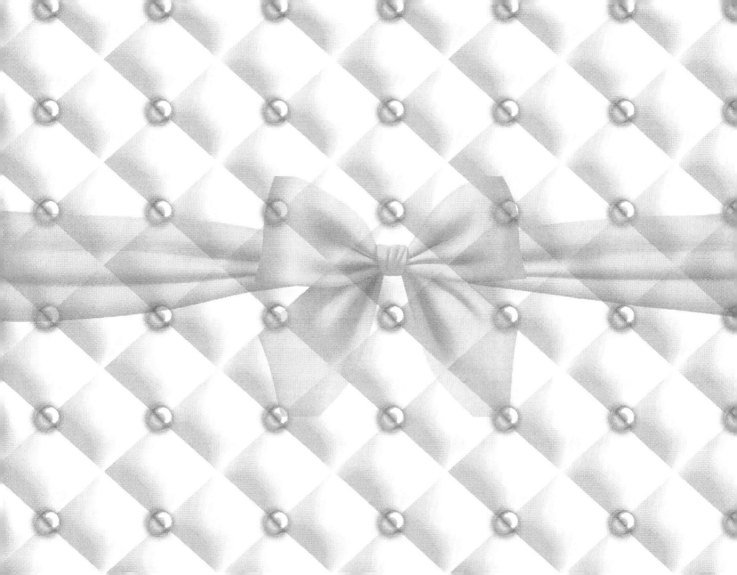

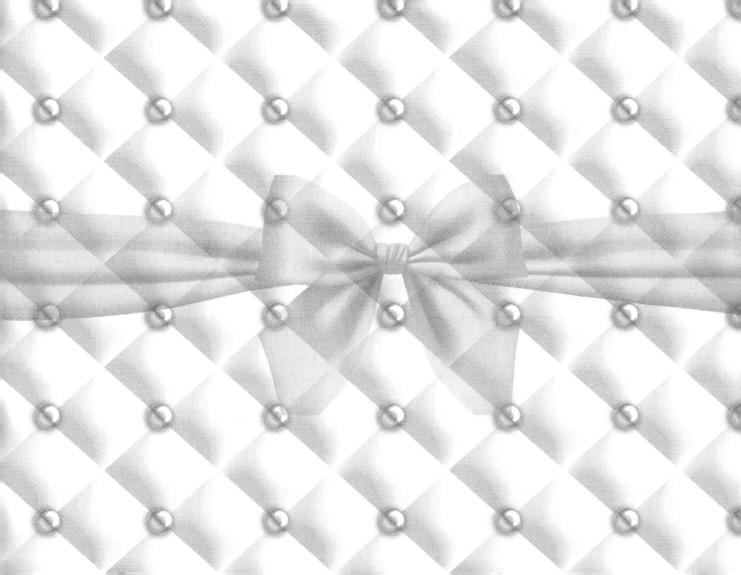

GOOD FOR ONE

NECK
&
EARLOBE

KISSES

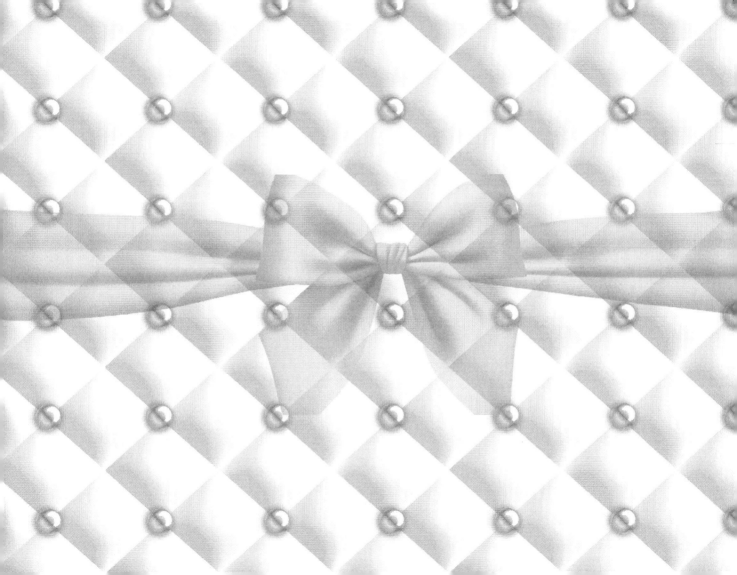

GOOD FOR ONE

I REALLY WANT TO

KISS YOU

AND NOT

JUST ON THE LIPS

GOOD FOR ONE

A HAWAIIAN

STRIP TEASE

GOOD FOR ONE

FINDING

THE G-SPOT

ORGASM

GOOD FOR ONE

CANDLELIT

BUBBLE BATH

GOOD FOR ONE

MY

SEXIEST FANTASY

PLAYED OUT RIGHT

IN FRONT

OF ME

GOOD FOR ONE

SENSUAL LAP

DANCE

GOOD FOR ONE

GET THE COCONUT OIL OUT IT'S ABOUT TO GET REAL FILTHY LAY ON YOUR TUMMY WHILE I OIL UP YOUR

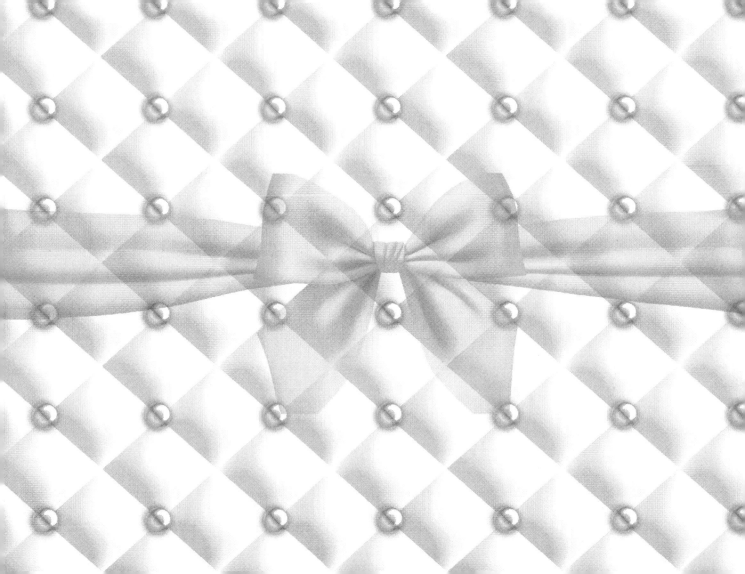

GOOD FOR ONE

PICK A FANTASY

ROLEPLAY

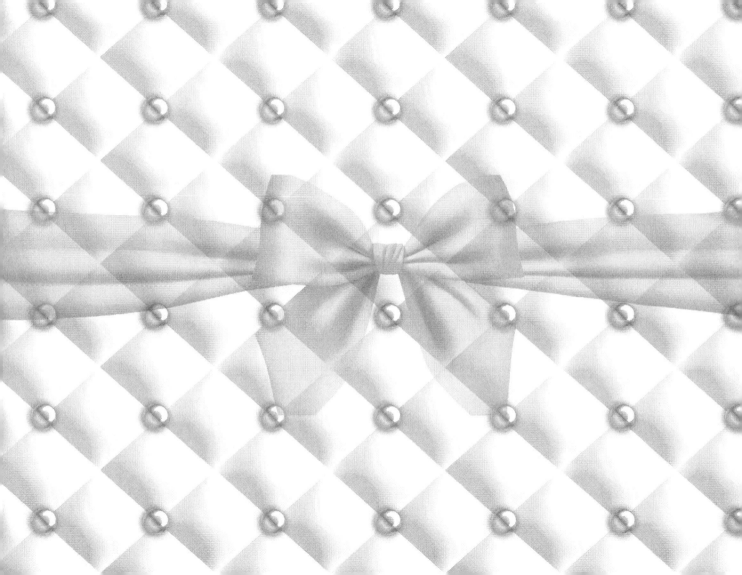

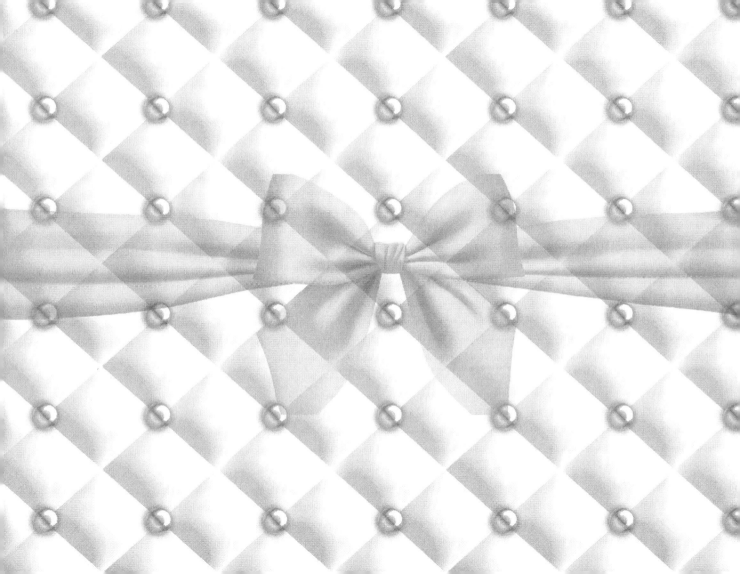

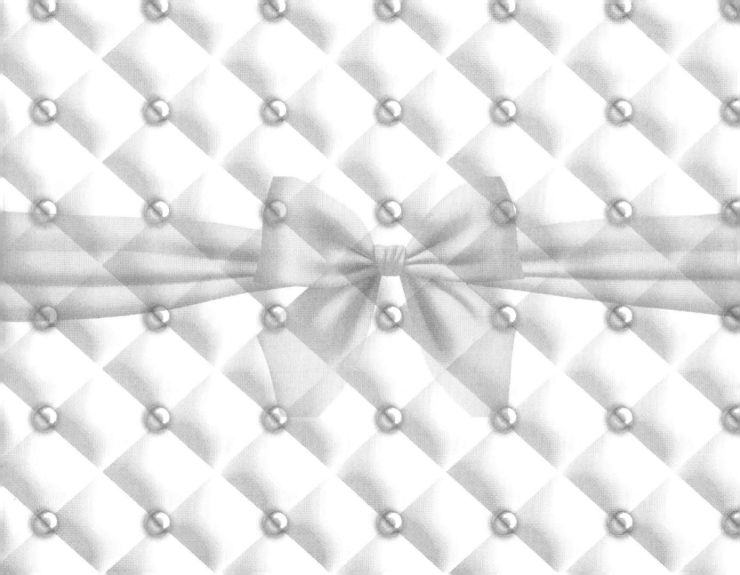

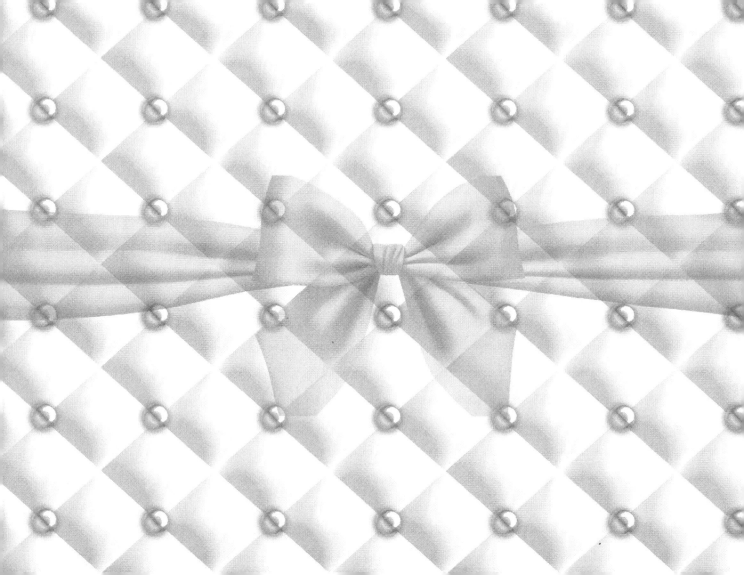

GOOD FOR ONE

TALKING DIRTY ALL THE NIGHT

GOOD FOR ONE

HAVE SHADES
OF
WHATEVER
SEX

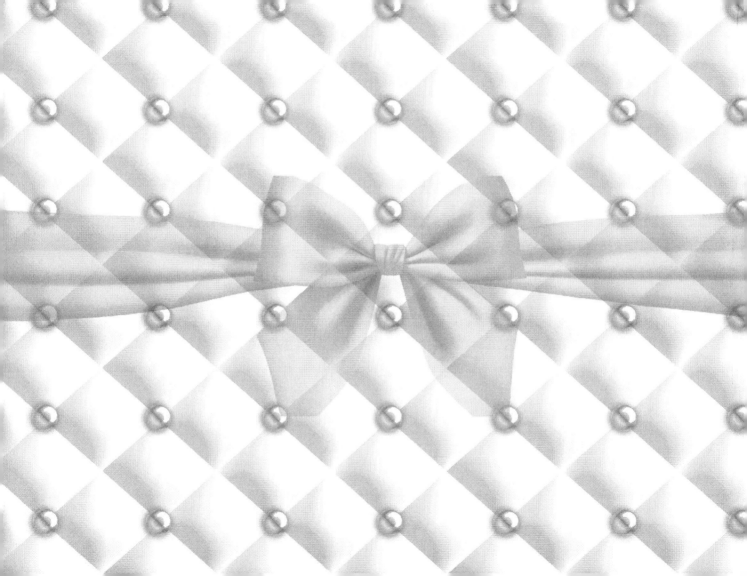

GOOD FOR ONE

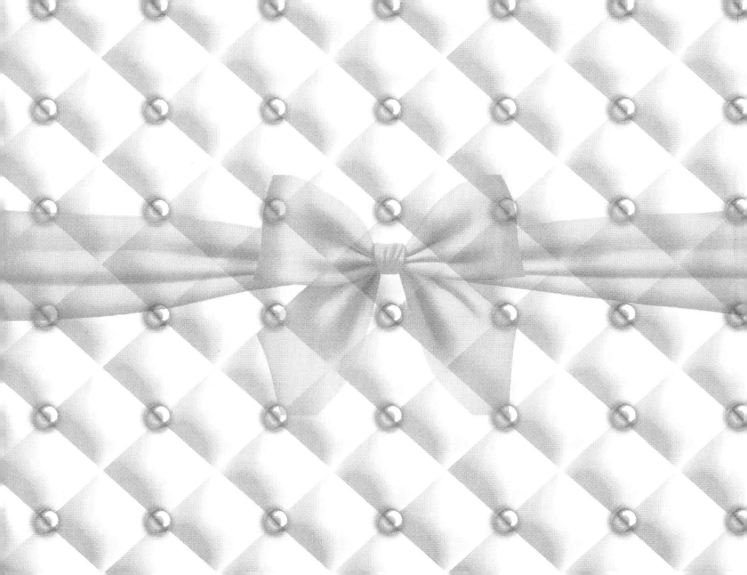

GOOD FOR ONE

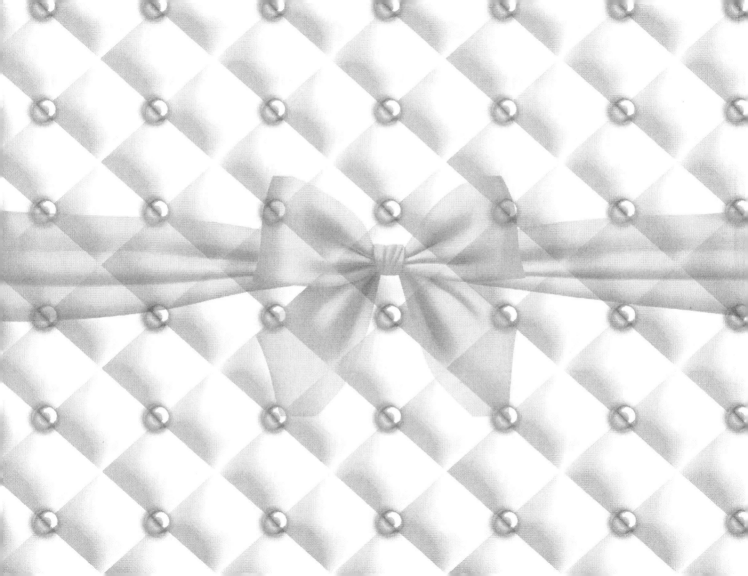

GOOD FOR ONE

Printed in Great Britain
by Amazon

12012520R00063